One Night

Bumble the bee went out for a stroll. He loved looking at the stars. That was his favorite thing about the night. He flied through the whole night not knowing were he was going.

He saw Something

he saw a beautiful creature. It was a butterfly bumble the bee got very excited he couldn't wait to play with the butterfly. Bumble the bee flew to the butterfly.

BUZZ...BUZZ...BUZZ

The Butterfly was Happy

when she saw the bee, they talked and talked all through the night. Bumble was very happy he made a new friend and so was the butterfly.

Bumble went Home

to tell everyone about his new friend. He flew as fast as he could so he could tell everyone about butterfly.

Bumble came Home

and told everyone about his new friend. Everyone was shocked they told Bumble he couldn't be friends with a butterfly. They are to different everyone told him. Bumble tried to tell them that butterflies are just like us, but no one listened

BUZZ...BUZZ...BUZZ

Bumble came to tell

butterfly about what the rest of the bees thought. Butterfly

was very sad, so she flew away and so did bumble they

were very sad they couldn't be friends.

Bumble and the bee's

were flying to a flower patch. Bumble was still very sad that he couldn't be friends with butterfly. He didn't know what to do.

A Bird Swiped

Bumble away all the bee's chased after the bird, but it was of no use. They tried and tried, but they couldn't save Bumble the bird flew higher and higher.

Butterfly comes and

saves bumble the bee, everyone is shocked that a butterfly saved a bumble bee. All the bee's told bumble bee and butterfly to go see the bee queen. Bumble was scared he thought he was in trouble.

The Queen Bee

was very happy with butterfly and Bumble. She said from now on Bees and Butterfly's are one. She even asked them if they can tell everyone at the party Queen Bee is holding.

Bumble and Butterfly

were at the ceremony were they were giving out the speech. They were very excited to do so. Everyone was there butterflies and bees. Even the Queen Bee was there, but no Butterfly king.

After the Speech

Bumble and Butterfly went to find the butterfly king. Where could he be Bumble thought. They had already checked all over the stadium, so where could he be.

Bumble and Butterfly

split up. Bumble checked the flower fields, but butterfly king

wasn't there.

Butterfly Checked

the kings tree, but the king wasn't there. Butterfly was

getting worried where could the king be.

Bumble even Checked

the honey pot, but like last time there was no king to be seen now even bumble was getting really worried.

Bumble and Butterfly

meet at the stadium and asked the queen bee if the king

had come here. The Queen laughed and told them that

the King was on vacation. Bumble and Butterfly started

laughing.

Bumble and Butterfly

went back on stage and continued their speech and everyone loved it. They were very happy to see that.

THE END

PicMonkey

This Book Is Dedicated To
Mom and Dad

Bumble The Bee